Tao of the Defiant Woman

FIVE BRAZEN WAYS TO ACCEPT WHAT YOU MUST AND REBEL AGAINST THE REST

To Melody,
Keep following your path with joy and vitality — Tao and defiance —
Best,
CJ

Tao of the Defiant Woman

FIVE BRAZEN WAYS TO ACCEPT WHAT YOU MUST AND REBEL AGAINST THE REST

CJ GOLDEN

SOURCEBOOKS, INC.®
NAPERVILLE, ILLINOIS

Published by Sourcebooks, Inc.
P.O. Box 4410, Naperville, Illinois 60567–4410
(630) 961–3900
Fax: (630) 961–2168
www.sourcebooks.com

Originally published in 2005.

Library of Congress Cataloging-in-Publication Data

Golden, C. J.
Tao of the Defiant Woman : Five Brazen Ways to Accept What You Must and Rebel against the Rest / CJ Golden.
p. cm.
ISBN 978-1-4022-1018-1 (trade pbk.)
1. Women--Life skills guides. 2. Women--Conduct of life. 3. Self-realization in women. I. Title.

HQ1221.G698 2007
155.6'33--dc22

2007020929

Printed and bound in the United States of America.
VP 10 9 8 7 6 5 4 3 2

For Joe.
You've made my life a wondrous adventure.

Acknowledgments

I would like to acknowledge those individuals who have helped me find peace and understanding as I travel down my own path.

Kathy Levinson, you gave me the inspiration and courage to begin this process, and for that I will always be grateful.

In large measure this book would never have happened had it not been for Jamie Callan, who contributed to this project from the very start. Without her help and guidance, The *Tao of the Defiant Woman* would never have found the light of day. You will see her work scattered throughout the chapters, especially in the very moving blessing at the end of the book. Thank you, Jamie, for your support and for allowing me to use some of your words and ideas in creating this text.

I owe a big debt of gratitude to my friends and family who have always provided the shoulder against which I could laugh or cry. Thank you for allowing me to share my dreams and desires with you all.

Mostly, however, I thank Joe, my wonderful husband, who insisted that I was a writer and supported me every inch of the way— both as a person and as an author; and my children and their spouses, David and Jessica, Donna and Steve,

Ami and Andy, and Beth. You have all stood by me with patience and encouragement as I faced my struggles. You never gave up, so I couldn't either.

I am forever thankful to Deb Werksman, my amazing editor at Sourcebooks, for seeing the value of this project and taking it on with enthusiasm and energy. My appreciation, as well, goes to all the folks at Sourcebooks for believing in this book, and especially Susie Benton for keeping me on target and organized.

Alix, Emily, and Josh, my remarkable grandchildren: one day you will understand that you are the reason I have grown to be content and strong. You have shown me how to follow the Tao of the Defiant Woman.

And lastly, to Jane—who taught me how important it is to do so.

Contents

Chapter 1

The Tao of Defiance

Tao (pronounced dow):

THE ANCIENT CHINESE PHILOSOPHY BEST TRANSLATED AS THE WAY OR THE PATH. IN MODERN TERMS, ONE MIGHT SAY IT MEANS GOING WITH THE FLOW.

Defiant:

REBELLIOUS AND BOLD.

By definition these two words would appear to be mutually exclusive. But this is not necessarily true.

Certainly, there are those women who, in their practice of Taoism, exude serenity. They recognize that they are one with nature, accepting their life's transitions as a part of that natural order. And there are others who, with their defiant attitude, seem to contest the inevitable changes that occur as they pass from one year to the next. But a combination of these two approaches is not impossible. Far from it, it is absolutely the healthiest and happiest mindset women can have.

I'm convinced that all women, especially as we approach our fourth, fifth, and sixth decades and beyond, can and should absolutely define ourselves as "Tao-and-Defiant." Those who do so are the most fully alive and contented women around. They're a joy to be with because they're completely comfortable with themselves, no matter what stage of their lives they happen to be in.

Women of today inevitably face various stumbling blocks and detours along our paths. Life does not always flow smoothly, but even when it does, we find ourselves confronted with the challenges of physical and emotional upheaval and unexpected lifestyle changes.

Transitions appear in our personal lives as we find our bodies changing both in appearance and in health; in our interpersonal lives—affecting our relationships with parents and children, husbands and lovers, friends and acquaintances; and in the world that surrounds us as we deal with jobs and careers, technological advances, demands on our leisure time, and revolutions in the arts, music, and fashion.

We are ever-evolving; our lives are constantly in flux. It is imperative that we find a way to handle these transitions contentedly, joyfully, and without regrets. We travel down life's path and discover that nothing remains the same. Nature changes: rivers flow over smooth soil and rocky boulders. Leaves turn from bright green to orange, red, and gold. The petals on a flower open from a bud, bloom, and ultimately fall. We're part of nature. We too change.

The woman who understands Tao recognizes that those transitions are to be expected and are going to occur and that, well, there's no use fighting them. Just watch that river as it makes its way downstream. There it is, flowing along calmly and effortlessly, when a large obstruction appears in its path. Okay, so the going gets rough for a bit, but eventually it finds smooth sailing again and continues gently on its way.

For those of you who are unfamiliar with Taoism, I'd like to introduce you to this amazing Eastern philosophy, putting it into the context of our lives today. Taoism offers us a path to follow as we go through the stages of our lives, existing in accord with nature's cycles. These transitions—many of which bring us new challenges from day to day—are part of that natural flow. Why, then, should we bemoan the passing from one phase of life to another?

It would take a lifetime of study to fully understand Taoism, and that is not the objective of this book. I am not suggesting that you embrace it as your value system, unless you find you would like to do so. What I am suggesting is that a rudimentary understanding of its principles will help you deal with the transitions you face as you negotiate your way through life.

This, then, is a modified Taoism 101 tutorial.

Yin and Yang

ALL LIFE EMBODIES YIN AND EMBRACES YANG, THROUGH THEIR UNION ACHIEVING HARMONY.
—TAO TE CHING

We begin with the yin and the yang, the world and its opposites. The yin is the female, the dark, the passive; the yang, or the male, is the light, the assertive. These two forces create each other, as the Tao Te Ching explains so beautifully:

Being and non-being create each other.
Difficult and easy support each other.

Long and short define each other.
High and low depend on each other.

Opposites, therefore, are inseparable and form the philosophy of unity that underlies Taoism.

Even as we know day and night, highs and lows, old and young, and sickness and health, we must learn to accept and appreciate each as a necessity for the other. The flip side of each—yin or yang—is not a positive or negative in itself, but allows us to realize the potential within the other.

Think about this for a moment. The cute black-and-white circular design we often see on Taoist T-shirts, mugs, and greeting cards, which signifies the yin and the yang, shows the two interlocking halves combining to make a whole. The world is made up of these opposing halves. So too are our lives. This is a fact of nature that, when fully acknowledged, aids us in our acceptance of life's ups and downs. Every day is not upbeat and positive, but we realize that these darker phases will serve to increase our appreciation for the more joyful times. And they may even lead to a new and constructive path on our journeys.

Take the story of Janet, a friend who is familiar with the way of the Tao. Stricken with the flu at one point three years ago, she found herself bedridden—too weak with aches and fever to go to work, visit with friends, or even enjoy a daytime TV show. Naturally a productive and energetic woman, Janet spent the first two days in bed inwardly griping about her situation. By day three, however, she recognized that she could either continue to grumble or find the flip side and turn the situation into something positive. Grabbing her journal and pen, Janet began to put on paper an idea she had been thinking about for several months. She had wanted to write a stage play based on the fascinating life of her immigrant grandfather but had never had enough time during her hectic, healthy days. Now she had nothing but time. It took but a day to complete—written entirely by hand in her journal as she lay in bed.

Janet's play was ultimately transcribed into manuscript form and submitted to a prestigious writing contest. And it was a winner—as was she.

Janet's story embodies the workings of yin and yang. She took a negative situation, found its flip side, and turned the episode into a positive life experience.

Tzu-Jan ("By Itself So")

OPEN YOURSELF TO THE TAO
AND TRUST YOUR NATURAL RESPONSES;
AND EVERYTHING WILL FALL INTO PLACE.
—TAO TE CHING

Tzu-jan, or "by itself so," refers to the fact that the flow of nature happens of its own accord, and we are an integral part of the universe and the cycles of life. When we accept this, we are able to live in greater harmony with nature, spontaneously and without inhibitions, content with each new year and stage. Just as we see spring turn to summer, summer to autumn, and autumn to winter, so too do our lives follow a natural path.

The autumn leaves fall from their branches to return the next spring. The trees do not suddenly decide, "I know what . . . Let's shake off our leaves." This all happens on its own, in accord with the laws of nature.

So too should we continue on our way through life's phases. Recognizing our oneness with the world around us helps us to accept our transitions comfortably and with grace.

I first met a woman named Muriel when she was in her mid-sixties. Charming and well educated, she was, nonetheless, very unhappy.

"I feel invisible," she said. "No one wants to talk to me; no one looks at me. I'm just, well, invisible." As she spoke, a look of despair passed over her otherwise lovely face. If this was the way she presented herself to the world—withdrawn and unhappy in her own being—it was no wonder she felt invisible. Think about the people to whom you are drawn. They are those who appear dynamic, interesting, and thoughtful. Muriel, on the other hand, appeared cold and unfriendly.

And just why was she behaving this way? Muriel was mourning the passing of her youth. Now older than the new personnel at the company where she worked, she began to compare herself with the women who were twenty or more years her junior. She compared her physical appearance and energy level with theirs. And in her mind, she came out on the short end. Had Muriel been able to note the comparisons of mind and life-learned skills, she would have given herself more credit for those years she has lived rather than denouncing herself for them.

I suggested that Muriel seek out women who were enjoying their journey down life's path, that she talk to them and really listen to what they could teach her about acceptance of oneself in spite of, and because of, their years. Through these conversations and the continued support of the women from whom she sought guidance, Muriel began to learn that physical changes reflect a life richly lived.

As she observed others who were enjoying their journey, she too began to accept that change is part of life. And one day, Muriel admitted she was actually beginning to enjoy the ride. Of course, with this newborn acceptance came an unconscious change in her bearing. Instead of sulking around the office, she began to walk with more confidence. This, in turn, brought about an openness in her personality that attracted others to her. Muriel began to take pride in who she was and where she was in her life. Now when she compares herself with her coworkers, she focuses on the positive attributes about herself and finds absolutely nothing at all negative.

Muriel now truly embodies *tzu-jan*—a woman whose beauty and intelligence shines brightly. And she is far from invisible.

Wu Wei ("Not Forcing")

THE MASTER ALLOWS THINGS TO HAPPEN . . .
SHE STEPS OUT OF THE WAY
AND LETS THE TAO SPEAK FOR ITSELF.
—TAO TE CHING

Wu wei, which translates into "not forcing," is the Taoist way of reminding us to go with the flow, to accept what we cannot change and do the best with what we are given. Picture a woman on an airplane traveling from New York to California. There she is, going from East to West, when all of a sudden she realizes that she left her makeup back in her Manhattan apartment. There's no way can she rush up to the pilot and insist the plane be returned to Kennedy Airport so that she can hop off and get her beauty supplies.

She cannot force the situation to be anything

other than what it is: she is going to arrive in Los Angeles without her mascara and lipstick. No amount of angst will change that fact. What she can do, however, is enjoy a cocktail or the in-flight movie and try to relax, sans makeup. Then, at her destination, she can go to the nearest department store cosmetics counter and purchase more.

Is this a frivolous example? Sure it is. But you get the picture—we need to understand that we cannot change that which is set by nature. By allowing our paths to flow in the direction intended, we relieve ourselves of unnecessary stress. Certainly Taoism does not recommend giving in or giving up; however, it does advocate making the most of each situation in our lives without forcing matters to an unnatural and painful conclusion.

The Tao teaches resilience. We are not expected to be complacent on our journeys. Rather, like the woman on the plane, we need to make the most of each situation as we follow *wu wei*.

Te ("Virtue")

WHEN YOU ARE CONTENT TO BE SIMPLY YOURSELF AND DON'T COMPARE OR COMPETE, EVERYBODY WILL RESPECT YOU.

—TAO TE CHING

Te, meaning "virtue," does not relate to being "good" in terms of behavior, but rather to being good at the skill of living. Everything in nature possesses an individuality that sets it apart from all others.

Recognizing that we are unique, we should follow our natural instincts and not allow others to force their expectations upon us. Nor should we impose ours on anyone else.

Consider the following passage from one of

the great communicators of Taoist thought, Chuang-tse. Perhaps it will further clarify the true meaning of *te*:

> *In the Age of Perfect Virtue, men lived among the animals and birds as members of one large family. There were no distinctions between "superior" and "inferior" to separate one man or species from another. All retained their natural Virtue and lived in the state of pure simplicity. . . .*
>
> *In the Age of Perfect Virtue, wisdom and ability were not singled out as extraordinary. The wise were seen merely as higher branches on humanity's tree, growing a little closer to the sun. People behaved correctly, without knowing that to be Righteousness and Propriety. They loved and respected each other, without calling that Benevolence. They were faithful and honest, without considering that*

to be Loyalty. They kept their word, without thinking of Good Faith. In their everyday conduct, they helped and employed each other, without considering Duty. They did not concern themselves with Justice, as there was no in*justice. Living in harmony with themselves, each other, and the world, their actions left no trace, and so we have no physical record of their existence.*

(Translation by Benjamin Hoff, The Te of Piglet*)*

Perhaps we can help to bring about a rebirth of the Age of Perfect Virtue beginning with ourselves. Not only should we respect those around us, but we also need to learn to respect ourselves—no matter our physical appearance, age, stage in our lives, abilities, or marital or job situation. That is surely the way to live virtuously, honestly, and truly fulfilled.

A thorough study of Taoism shows that it is

not a passive philosophy. Although we recognize change as inevitable, the Tao does not teach that we give up or give in; rather, we accept our new situations and then react accordingly. This is where defiance enters the picture.

Behaving in a defiant manner does not, in this case, mean stamping your feet and shouting "no!" like a petulant child who refuses to take a much-needed nap. Defiance does not mean shaving off your hair just because you begin to notice that it's more gray than blond. Nor does it suggest locking yourself in the house and refusing to come out when the man you love has moved on and in with someone else.

The defiant woman I wish to depict is a gal who looks at her situation, recognizes and accepts those parts that cannot be changed, and then goes ahead and challenges those that she can improve. This woman will look in the mirror, observe the signs of passing time, and realize it's all part of life. Then, rather than bemoaning her "fate," she will either embrace her lines and evolving hair color or enhance them—slightly. She will not feel the need to look ten or twenty years younger.

This woman who is both Tao and defiant might one day find herself facing mandatory retirement from a job she has worked at her entire adult life. Perhaps she has given up the possibility of marriage and motherhood for this career. She might try to fight the system; perhaps her bosses will allow her to remain longer. She may be told she has to leave, and that is a very painful thing to hear. Yet she understands she is still vibrant and viable and has much to offer to others. Her Tao mindset will allow her to accept the obligatory good-bye party and gold watch. The defiant part of her personality will spur her to find another outlet for her energy and abilities. She will not give up or give in. This woman will, instead, forge ahead as she follows the path of her life with all of its twists and turns.

Recently I had the pleasure of connecting with Judith, a former colleague. As we chatted about the many years since our last meeting, I listened attentively while she spoke of her children and grandchildren, her former marriages, her shoulder and knee-replacement surgeries, her retirement job at a nursing facility, and her approaching seventieth birthday. She then produced two photographs that, I assumed, were going to allow me a glimpse of those grandchildren she was so very proud of. Was I ever wrong! The pictures Judith shared with me featured the face of a woman who was grinning ear to ear in midair during her first parachute jump.

"It was amazing," she said, "something I'd always wanted to do."

The best part of Judith's story was her

description of the looks of incredulity she received from the younger women standing with her as they waited to get into the plane that would take them two miles up into the air. They couldn't believe this older woman was actually part of the group. Judith was certainly being defiant in the true sense of the word—she was defying the expectations of those around her.

We spoke of her motorcycle rides in Bermuda, her yearning to parasail, and the recent rose tattoo she sported on her ankle.

"When I was younger," she said, "I had to be more careful, not take as many risks. After all, I was responsible for the care of my children and some of the grandchildren. As I see it, now it's my turn."

At a time in her life when many others begin to take fewer risks, Judith took on fresh challenges every year. Her life contrasts sharply with that of so many women who, as they grow older, allow their lives to shrink. New fears creep in, and they become sedentary, finding that their worlds are smaller and smaller. I have always believed that we must continue to learn and explore all of our possibilities. Rather than retreating to a life of diminishing activities, we should make a point of expanding our catalog of experiences every year. How exciting it is to reflect back on a year where we have learned a new skill, taken part in a great adventure, or accomplished some exciting mission.

There I was, having lunch with a woman who truly epitomized the term Tao-and-Defiant. Certainly Judith has been through her share of life's ups and downs. Yet with the combined attitudes of acceptance and defiance, she continues to live a life of joy and fulfillment.

Just as Taoism follows several core principles, so too does the woman who is both Tao and defiant. But she has a set uniquely her own.

The Five Principles of the Tao of the Defiant Woman:

1. The defiant woman recognizes that her body is changing, and she is thankful that it continues to work as well as it does.
2. The defiant woman understands that her relationships are ever-evolving, and she accepts that, for she knows she's a work in progress too.
3. The defiant woman treasures her friends and draws strength from the community of women.
4. The defiant woman seeks positive role models to help guide her and strives to be a like example for her daughters.
5. The defiant woman knows that the world around her continues to develop and is content, because there is always something new and exciting to learn.

As the stages of our lives come and go, if we can strive to remember the lessons of Taoism while incorporating a necessary element of defiance, I propose that women will become healthier and happier on our journey through life.

And just who is this, coaching you on following the Tao of the Defiant Woman? I'm a woman who embraces Taoism to help me on my journey, and one who takes delight in challenging life's transitions. I'm a spiritual person who embraces the Tao as a philosophy of life, yet I maintain an adventurous and defiant streak. I'm a woman who holds on to my girlish sense of joy and wonder.

I personify a woman who follows the principles of the Tao of the Defiant Woman, and I would like to be your guide and mentor as we work our way together through the ideas and reflections that follow.

My sincerest wish is that you come away from this experience with an enhanced appreciation for your life and yourself and, like me, recognize the strength and joy in following the Tao of the Defiant Woman.

Chapter 2
Five Principles to Defy By

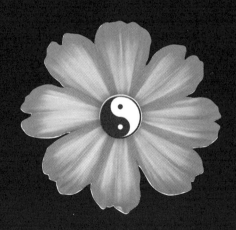

Principle One

The defiant woman recognizes that her body is changing, and she is thankful that it continues to work as well as it does.

✻***As we get older, our metabolisms shift and our hips change shape. We can defy some of these changes, but at some point, we must accept our body's changes as a fact of life and see the beauty in all its various changes.***✻

—Don't Sweat the Small Stuff *daily calendar*

Cosmetic surgery—it's all the rage lately. Why? Because our bodies are changing. Our podiatrists may offer us orthotics for our shoes to support our now flatter arches; the once smooth skin on our legs and hips may now harbor areas of cellulite; and our weight and height changes might appear diametrically opposed to each other, as we gain in pounds but shrink in inches. Peering into the mirror, we notice pesky signs of aging, such as laugh lines deepening around our eyes and mouth.

This is the picture of a woman following the path of life. She, like all things in the universe, is changing. Like a leaf in autumn—that intricate piece of nature's art that has shifted from vibrant green to gold, red, and orange—she too is beautiful. Like all living beings, that leaf is following its path of life. And it is all beautiful.

When we were young girls, each physical change represented growth and maturation—and how exciting it all was! Do you remember the day you were putting on your pajamas and noticed the beginnings of breasts? Or when you could no longer wear children's jeans because they would not fit around your newly rounded hips?

Why is it that we now separate ourselves from nature and regard our physical changes so negatively? Could it be because this is what our culture teaches us? Those who live elsewhere in the world, those who embrace life's journey, recognize the joy in such transformations. After all, it represents our growth and the gift of continued life.

Let me share with you a story that exemplifies the Taoist attitude toward physical alterations:

> *There was a famous acolyte traveling around the countryside seeking the wisdom to live well and properly. One day he came upon an old woman, hunched and shriveled with age. Although she was bent and withered, her skin was amazingly youthful.*
>
> *The student looked at her closely and then said, "Excuse me. I don't mean to intrude, but you are so old in years, yet your complexion is like that of a child. How is this so?"*
>
> *"Oh," the old woman said, laughing easily, "I suppose that is because I follow the Way."*

This old woman, so accepting of the flow of nature, had no need to disguise her age through physical modifications. She did not feel discontented with, or inhibited by, her aging body. Quite the contrary—her complexion, which was "like that of a child," reflected the serenity within her soul.

So many women buy into our culture's incorrect and impossible manifestation of the perfect body, the perfect weight, the perfect shape. We open popular magazines and find photos of actresses and models who are impossibly thin and beautiful. And we idolize them for these attributes—and disdain our own bodies for not following suit. What we refuse to consider is that most of these women have to force their bodies into these shapes. They spend hours each day with their personal trainers or follow strict diets to keep their weight down. I will admit that working out and watching one's food intake is healthy, but not to the stressful extent undertaken by these women.

Often their pictures are airbrushed and doctored to diminish their "flaws." Do you remember Doris Day? She was a charming singer and actress from the 1940s and 1950s who, when photographed, was placed in a soft light that hid the abundance of freckles on her sweet face. How sad that those freckles were considered unsightly enough that they needed to be swept away by lighting.

Some women are genetically blessed—or so we believe them to be. Yet even the tall often yearn to be shorter, and the slim complain that they are too skinny. And those who wish themselves into unattainable shapes remain discontented. We are all genetically blessed: we have our own wonderful bodies, whatever size and shape they might come in.

But many women are unhappy with their

looks and have made decisions based on that unhappiness.

WHEN PEOPLE SEE SOME THINGS AS BEAUTIFUL,
OTHER THINGS BECOME UGLY.
WHEN PEOPLE SEE SOME THINGS AS GOOD,
OTHER THINGS BECOME BAD.

—TAO TE CHING

Instead of looking in the mirror with disdain, I want you to learn to embrace what you see and recognize the beauty of that image. Your reflection, after all, is merely the shell that envelops the person within. Perhaps the shell has gained more weight than you would have wished, but if your spirit is beautiful, how can your body be otherwise?

If that weight gain was a result of a health issue, such as hypothyroidism, you need to accept that newly voluptuous body.

If those extra pounds are a result of overindulgence, well then allow yourself the pleasurable memory of all those grande mocha caffe lattes, and stop berating yourself for enjoying them. And take the necessary steps to trim down for the sake of your health.

I do not sanction gorging yourself on donuts and, thus, watching the numbers on your scale rise every day. This is unhealthy, and we should refuse to use *wu wei* or *tzu-jan* as an excuse to do ourselves harm! But disparaging ourselves for those excess pounds will not help the situation. Nor will ignoring the fact by avoiding mirrors, hiding the scale, and wearing oversized, loose clothing. However you deal with the situation, do not ever fall into the trap of disliking your body. To do so would be to dislike your very being. First and foremost, love yourself and your body. Only then will you want to take care of it and present yourself to the world as confident and proud. And, I promise, then you will glow with a radiant beauty that transcends the mere physical.

Taking joy in life is a woman's best cosmetic.

—*Rosalind Russell*

So why the current obsession with cosmetic surgery? Is this how the woman who is both Tao and defiant changes her appearance for the better? No, not necessarily.

The way you can demonstrate your defiance and improve your appearance is by using a magical tool called attitude, by embracing your looks—wrinkles and all—and by being proud of your body, whatever shape it is in. By sending this message of confidence out into the world, you begin to alter other people's perceptions of beauty as well.

What is the sixty-year-old woman teaching

the twenty-year-old about physical appearance when she shuns her hard-won smile lines and resorts to a face-lift? How apprehensive will that younger woman feel about her future looks, when she knows so many older women are rushing off to the cosmetic surgeon to have liposuction, eye lifts, and tummy tucks? The lesson that younger woman is learning is that she must do all she can to avoid such "unsightly features" as a double chin, crow's-feet, and a bulging midsection.

I'm not reproaching the remarkable work being done by today's cosmetic surgeons. Nor am I suggesting that women never take advantage of these amazing accomplishments. But though not denouncing cosmetic surgery procedures, the defiant woman recognizes that they serve to change or enhance the outer shell only. Her self-worth and, therefore, her true beauty, come from within.

Go ahead—have liposuction or a face-lift if you truly desire, but please remember that the effect of cosmetic intervention is only superficial and that those who truly care about you recognize your inner beauty and essence regardless of one or two new lines or chins that might appear.

I challenge you to ask those who love you whether you should go under the knife—and see what their replies are. I believe you'll be surprised more often than not and will have cause to reconsider.

I issued this same challenge to my friend, Annette:

"People kept telling me I was so pretty, but I knew they couldn't be right," she said. "I have these wrinkles between my eyebrows, and the bags under my eyes just made me look awful." When I suggested that Annette ask her husband, children, and two best friends for their

honest opinion about her receiving Botox injections, she said she was sure they'd agree that it was the best thing for her to do.

"Why on earth would you want to do that?" they all responded. "What wrinkles are you talking about? Bags under your eyes? Where?"

It seemed that only Annette focused in on what she considered her major imperfections. Those who knew and loved her saw only her radiant smile and charming personality.

I hate to say "I told you so," but Annette, I told you so.

Sometimes you can't see yourself clearly until you see yourself through the eyes of others.

—Ellen DeGeneres

As a defiant woman who also follows a Taoist philosophy, you accept—you love—your physical appearance. If, for health reasons, you need to lose or gain weight, you will do so. But you won't allow yourself to fall into the "I've got to diet/gain because I'm so ugly this way" trap. Your mindset will be "I will lose/gain the necessary amount of weight to take the best care possible of my exceptional body."

As a Tao-and-Defiant woman, you embrace the face you see each day in the mirror, with all of its special features, smile lines, and wrinkles.

While our bodies and faces are busy transforming themselves, we may also change in other, more significant physical ways. The state of our health may diminish: our muscles weaken, our immune systems wane, we become less resilient, and our hormones play tricks on us. This is all a natural part of the process of being one with nature.

Right now, you might be shaking your head and thinking that this "being one with nature" business can be a bit disheartening. It is definitely not fun to find your body incapable of performing as it once did. You might have suffered an accident and injured your leg or neck or back; perhaps you are now dealing with a difficult health issue. Maybe the passing years have stolen some of your flexibility or strength; merely sitting in an air-conditioned restaurant in summer might have become a challenge as you fight off those hot flashes brought on by diminishing hormone levels. However, by making peace with your situation, you can rise above these setbacks. Your body has changed, but your being—your essence—remains uniquely yours.

Instead of "Why me?" and "I hate this . . . [you fill in the blank]," you can turn your thinking around to "Okay, this is me" and "I can deal with this." How? By fully embracing the mindset of the Tao-and-Defiant woman. It can be done. Women all around us provide living, breathing examples of this philosophy of acceptance and action.

Miriam, a woman I know, tore her rotator cuff during an overly enthusiastic game of basketball. Instead of putting her athletic lifestyle on hold during the healing process, she focused on sports that didn't require such rigorous use of her shoulder. She started jogging, an activity she hadn't pursued for several years, and remembered how much she had loved it. To make up for the social camaraderie that basketball had provided, Miriam enlisted several friends to join her on her morning jogs. And to keep in contact with her former basketball buddies, she continued attending the games—only this time as a cheerleader for her team.

Miriam accepted the limitations placed on her. She cannot help her teammates on the court this year and may never be able to do so again. However, she can get on with her life—

utilizing the strength of body and spirit available to her. Her Tao-and-Defiant philosophy of life keeps her on a positive path.

I have made it my goal to try a new physical activity each year. It is amazing, I have discovered, how far my limits can truly stretch. I've been following the examples of women I know and admire—women who have over the last few years learned how to golf, started playing basketball, participated in lengthy walks for charitable causes, and forced away fears by going hot-air ballooning or parasailing. These women refuse to allow the passing years and, perhaps, physical ailments to deter them. Sure, some have to visit their chiropractors on a more regular basis, but if doing so helps keep them limber enough to participate in such activities, those visits are well worth it. The important thing to remember is that as we grow older, we do not have to accept limitations. Our abilities may wane in one area, but there is always another direction that we can follow.

There are times when the actual, physical act of defiance is difficult to achieve. Because of injury, your body may have become weakened. The natural process of aging produces changes within you. How, then, does the defiant woman respond when physical infirmities or age-related adjustments occur? By continuing to live life to the fullest extent possible. By downplaying her limitations and focusing on her strengths. By showing the world her journey has not come to a dead end just because her direction has changed. New directions offer new courses to pursue, and the defiant woman pursues them with enthusiasm.

If your knees no longer allow you to jog, walk. When your back refuses to allow you to play at the club, swim. If you don't know how to swim, learn.

I fully realize that words written on a page like

this are merely that—just words. I can write them, and you can read them, but learning to live them may be a difficult task. Yet if you truly desire more contentment in your life, you are well on your way to becoming Tao-and-Defiant.

Please keep in mind the defiant women we've just discussed. Their Taoist spirit recognizes that as transformations and changes occur in their lives, acceptance is the key.

Taoism, which is not the same as complacency, allows you to avoid simply sitting back and accepting the curveballs life can throw. As that old saying goes, "When life gives you lemons, make lemonade." The defiant woman who lives by the Tao knows the truth of this maxim and does not fight her destiny. Instead, she works with it to the best of her ability to create within herself a joyous and accepting spirit.

As a Tao-and-Defiant woman, you deal with the physical detours along your path. They don't grind your journey to a halt, because you have strengths and attributes that will take over for those that need recharging. And you use those strengths to forge a new path—one that can be just as exhilarating and fulfilling as the last one was.

So get out there, and follow the Tao of the Defiant Woman:

Take on a new activity, one that emphasizes your strengths and downplays your limitations. Stretch your imagination and your boundaries: if you now walk, try in-line skating; if you cross-country ski, try alpine; if you ride a bike, try your grandkid's scooter; if you ballroom dance, try belly dancing.

If you prefer something less physical, help out at some sporting event; be a scorekeeper for a golf tournament; cheer on the athletes at a Special Olympics competition; help your town plan the next Labor Day parade. Whatever you do, share your abilities with others, and let them see you living your life with enthusiasm.

Jog joyfully down that path, knowing that no matter what physical changes come your way, you remain beautiful and vital. And when you live this way, you become a role model for others following you on this wonderful journey of life.

Our bodies change; there is no denying that fact. The Tao-and-Defiant woman is accepting of each physical transformation for she understands that her inner beauty and vitality continue to shine through for all to see.

I finally realized that being grateful to my body was key to giving more love to myself.

—*Oprah Winfrey*

Do you follow the Tao of the Defiant Woman in being thankful for your body?

1. **If you have ever gained or lost weight,**
   - How do the numbers on your scale make you feel about yourself?
   - If you're unhappy with your weight, what can you do to cut yourself some slack?
   - What can you do to show the world that size does not determine a woman's beauty?

2. **If you are dealing with a physical condition that is "cramping your style,"**
   - Are you able to accept it and ready to go on with your life?
   - How can you use *wu wei* (not forcing) and *tzu-jan* (going with the flow) to help?
   - What activities do you participate in that let the world know that you can still be defiant, regardless of physical setbacks?

3. When you look in the mirror,

- Do you embrace the person reflected back to you—regardless of and *because* of the changes from year to year?
- What can you do to help yourself realize how beautiful you truly are?
- If you are not totally happy with your appearance, what steps do you think I would suggest you take to "make it better"?

Principle Two

The defiant woman understands that her relationships are ever-evolving, and she accepts that, for she knows she's a work in progress too.

We turn not older with years,

but newer every day.

—Emily Dickinson

As we progress down the path of life, we are fortunate to have others around us to help us on the road: husbands or lovers, parents, children, extended family members, friends and acquaintances. And as we have learned, as our paths meander on, so too do these relationships. Significant others may leave us; parents pass on; children find their own roads and depart the nest—or return; colleagues move to other jobs and other towns; and we discover ourselves without them.

This is normal, albeit sometimes painful. The upside, however, is the fact that even as past relationships leave us or change, new ones enter our lives.

The defiant woman, following the Tao, accepts these changes, despite the fact that they often bring with them emotional upheavals—those boulders in the stream that the river inevitably encounters on its journey.

The story of Cinderella, who marries Prince Charming, is a wonderful fairy tale—the operative term here being "fairy tale." Sure, it would be wonderful to believe that after all the trials and tribulations Cinderella had to endure, her life remained stable and carefree from her wedding day on through to her time of "happily ever after." I bet that it didn't. Not that I'm claiming to know anything about life in the castle. Nor do I know anything about her Prince Charming husband and their relationship. But I would wager that she too faced the same challenges and transitions that we all do.

The problem is that as children, we are fed these fantastic stories, and all too often we expect them to translate into our own lives. We expect a happily ever after, and that is sometimes not the case. And we get very shaken up when things don't follow a smooth path.

Do you remember a childhood friend?

Someone with whom you shared your dolls and toys, who came to your house for sleepovers and stayed up late singing silly songs and giggling with you over childhood stories? Do you remember the day she told you her mommy and daddy were moving away and she had to leave you? If, like many of us, you can remember such an incident, then you remember one of the first disappointments in your young life—and one of the first lessons in relationships. They change. People, no matter how much you love them or how close you are to them, may just up and leave you. And that hurts.

Family or business commitments take your neighbors and friends from you and plant them elsewhere in the country. Of course, you claim that the geographical distance will never change your relationship, but that is unreasonable. You can certainly remain friends, but it will be different. You won't be able to go out for coffee together on a regular basis, but you can still share your lives over the phone or through the written word. You and your friend will not see each other as often, but you can make dates to visit each other. Maybe you can even plan a girls' weekend in some exotic locale away from both of your homes.

There are times, too, when you and your friend part ways, and it has nothing to do with geography. That's fine when you both recognize that the separation is for the best. An angry estrangement is painful. However, people come into our lives at various junctures to help us through a particular phase. Then we naturally drift apart. That's okay. We need not hold on to every friendship for all of our days. What we have to do, however, is remember these women and remain thankful to them for the time they were in our lives. And then we must let go.

On your wedding day, you and your

betrothed promised to love each other until "death do us part." Sometimes, however, you find that one or both of you change—you grow, mature, and become different people. Sometimes one or both of you fall out of love and realize that your future now holds the pain of divorce.

There are also those instances when "death do us part" becomes a reality, and that is the heartrending scenario that brings about the finality of your marriage.

We can stomp and cry and deny these facts forever, but doing so does not change the outcome. We are, for one reason or another, now unmarried—either a divorcée or widow—and it is within our power to accept the situation with all of its ramifications and continue on with our life in this new situation.

Of course, this brings about an extremely painful and difficult time. The emotional upheaval, which is often complicated by financial and personal uncertainties, creates one of the most stressful situations a human being has to contend with in life. This is when you need to allow the precepts of Taoism to enter into your mind and soul. Change happens, but life forges ahead. Our circumstances are altered, but our days continue nonetheless. And we can either accept this and work with what we have been dealt, or give up and die—emotionally, if not physically. It's tough, there's no doubt about that. It is at this moment, however, when your defiant attitude comes into play. You won't give up because there is still too much life ahead of you. And as long as you are here for the ride, you might as well embrace and enjoy it!

And what about our children—those wonderful little people whose lives we are entrusted to protect and nurture? We love them with all our hearts, teach them our value systems, and watch them grow into adults themselves. But ah, there's the rub—they grow into adults themselves, into thinking, decision-making people who have the nerve to want to lead lives of their own.

Sure, there were many times, especially during their teenage years, when you would have been more than happy if a UFO dropped out of the sky and whisked them away—they were often that infuriating. But you didn't really mean it when you thought that. Now they've decided to leave the nest and begin their own adventures.

And you miss them.

And perhaps you feel "unnecessary," for so much of your life has been devoted to them, and now they don't need you in the same way. Now what are you supposed to do with all those hours you used to spend driving them to their soccer games? The professors at college don't want you there for parent–teacher meetings.

Your children's social lives now happen without your approval—no more curfews and no permission needed for parties and dates.

No, you don't need to be the mommy anymore, but you are still very much a part of your children's lives. And you now have more time to spend on another very important relationship—with yourself. Remember all those activities you once wanted to pursue, if only you had the time? Well, now you've got a few spare hours, so go have some fun for yourself.

And as I mentioned before, as some relationships leave and change, so do new ones enter our lives. Those children who left the nest begin to construct nests of their very own. All of a sudden, you become a mother-in-law. Then, one day, you find yourself being referred to as Grandma. Hmm . . . now how did that happen?

I have met women who have a difficult time processing the fact that they are grandmothers.

After all, their own grandmothers were old ladies, which they are definitely not. Okay, so perhaps you are not old, and perhaps you are a grandmother. The title doesn't change who you are. It adds another layer to your multifaceted world of relationships and, in doing so, enriches your life. And you now have the opportunity to enrich the life of your grandchild.

As we journey down life's path, so too do others whom we love. Our parents grow older and more fragile. We are confronted with important decisions to make about their well-being, their health, and their economic security. Suddenly we find ourselves being their caretakers. We have become the parents, they the children. It's the ultimate role reversal. And one day, our children might have to do the same for us. This is the way of nature and a part of the journey that we may all have to face.

The Taoist recognizes the natural flow and

progression of these life events. Although some events happen of their own accord in harmony with nature—the maturation of our children, the aging of our parents, the birth of our grandchildren—others would seem to appear out of the blue. They are unexpected and possibly inexplicable. Yet these twists in the road happen, and we must be prepared to deal with them accordingly. That's where a degree of defiance comes in handy.

I am not insinuating that any of these events are easy to deal with. I don't have a quick fix for you as you confront and cope with such challenges as those I've just discussed.

There are no simple answers that you can find by reading a book—even this one. What I am suggesting is that you think about the principles of the Tao and add to that a "never give up" attitude. See how, together, the principles might work to better your situation and help you to understand your new role within these changed relationships.

Let's take a look at some of the natural transitions you might find yourself dealing with as you work your way through life. An example of what we've been discussing can be found in the story of my friend Millie.

Millie's life had always revolved around her husband and children—mostly her children. Carpool mom, PTA member, chief homework inspector, nutritionist, health care provider, head chef, cheerleader, and adviser, she defined herself by these roles. Not having a job outside of the home allowed Millie to expend all of her time and energy taking care of her family. And she relished that role.

Time passed, as it has a tendency to do, and one by one, her three children grew to adulthood, went off to college, and left their mother suffering a severe case of empty-nest syndrome.

She had no idea who she was anymore. And she felt completely useless: her children, she decided, really didn't need her anymore. She didn't consider that they would always need her, albeit in a different way. They were no longer little children who required chauffeuring from one place to another. Nor was she obliged to perform the daily caretaking tasks. Now they wanted her adult counsel, still as their mother, but also as their friend.

Once Millie recognized this, she embraced her new role in their lives. And ultimately, she realized that she now had time to find some other roles for herself—as her own person and not just as her children's mother.

As a Tao-and-Defiant woman, you, like Millie, need to come to terms with the changes you face as you journey down life's path. And you have to accept and make the most of these changes.

YOU CANNOT CHANGE THE WORLD,
BUT YOU CAN CHANGE THE WAY YOU REACT TO IT.

Your world will change, especially within that microcosm called your family. Not one of the relationships around you will remain static. Some adjustments, however, are more difficult to cope with than the one Millie faced. Even though they are as natural as any other transition in nature, they are always difficult and unexpected.

The day might come when you must exchange your child-caretaking duties for parent-caretaking efforts. How painful it is to go through this experience, to see your parents become debilitated, frail, helpless. And you will expend much time and energy making complex decisions about their health care and living conditions. There is no easy way to get through this.

However, I am urging you to hang onto your Taoist serenity. This is a boulder on your path, which you must now rise above. And the way to overcome it is with the knowledge that this time in your life will show you how powerful you really are. You will call upon reserves of physical, mental, and emotional strength that will make you proud of yourself.

Those deeply buried resources also rise to the surface when and if you suddenly find your formerly married self single again.

That "happily ever after" that concluded Cinderella's story does not happen for all of us. We all must know women who after many years (or perhaps only several months) of marriage faced divorce proceedings—or widowhood. Both experiences are equally painful in their own ways, and both require the Tao-and-Defiant woman to call upon all of her inner reserves.

As a Taoist, she first needs to accept the

situation. She is now single—with all of the ramifications this involves. There are financial considerations as well as emotional issues to cope with. These are real concerns that do indeed need to be faced. Wishing away the problems will not dissolve them. Nor will it ease the pain. This is where a woman's defiant attitude must take over.

The defiant woman who understands and accepts Taoism realizes that her life is not over. Yes, it is different and temporarily more difficult, perhaps. Maybe, if her newly acquired status of divorcée comes after years of a tumultuous marriage, her emotional life is now more peaceful. Either way, tomorrow will come, and how to deal with it is her decision alone.

One woman may curl up into a ball and sleepwalk through the rest of her days. Another might allow anger, disappointment, and hurt to overtake her psyche. I propose that women defy these negative attitudes and continue showing ourselves and the rest of the world just how strong we are. With that attitude firmly in mind, eventually we begin to believe in ourselves, continue on our paths, and find the joy that we deserve on our way.

One of the great truths of Taoism states:

TO CONDUCT ONE'S LIFE ACCORDING TO THE TAO IS TO CONDUCT ONE'S LIFE WITHOUT REGRETS AND TO REALIZE THE POTENTIAL WITHIN ONESELF.

Perhaps you are blessed with a strong will and can read these words, immediately apply them to your own life, and voilà, all is well in your world. That would, to say the least, thrill me to no end. How nice it would be if my coaching job were so simple. Well, as a mentor, I hope I am helping you. But we need to do more work together, and my most important task is to remind you of all the five principles of the Tao of the Defiant Woman. No single one of the five stands alone. In order for you to deal positively with the transitions that occur within the relationships we have just discussed, it is imperative that you remember each of the other principles on that list.

You must always remember that you are a beautiful and vibrant woman—no matter what particular role you perform within your relationships. Your body and beauty come from within your soul, and when that beauty radiates out into the world, you feel better about yourself. Only then can you feel more positive about your particular circumstances.

The Tao-and-Defiant woman seeks others who have successfully walked down similar paths. She models her behavior after those women and allows them to show her that all things are possible, no matter how bleak things might look at the present moment.

She remembers that the whole world is ever-changing, including her personal world. And she finds counsel in her community of friends. She allows them to aid her and draws comfort and joy from their companionship.

As our journeys through life evolve, so too do the relationships within our families. Parents, children, and lovers alike all grow and change. And so must we adjust to our new roles with each of them. In doing so, we truly remain a work in progress—joyfully recognizing this through our Tao-and-Defiant attitude.

The universe is change;
our life is what our thoughts make it.

—*Marcus Aurelius*

Do you follow the Tao of the Defiant Woman in accepting your changing relationships?

1. As your role with your children evolves,

- Do you remember that as adults your children still need you—just in a different way?
- Can you reinvent yourself and still fill your days now that you face an empty nest?
- Will you proudly show the world how vibrant a grandmother can be?

2. How about after "happily ever after"?

- What can you do to keep the joy in your marriage?
- If you find yourself divorced or widowed, what would I want you to do to remain vital and happy?
- How can you achieve this?

3. If your parents are elderly,

- Are you prepared to be the "parent" if that becomes necessary?
- If family demands on you become overwhelming, what can you do to help ease your own way?
- Will you remember to be proud of yourself for your strength during this difficult time?

Principle Three

The defiant woman treasures her friends and draws strength from the community of women.

Your wealth is where your friends are.

—*Plautus*

When talking about friendships, a very dear friend of mine, Jamie, uses the phrase "friendship feng shui." Feng shui is the theory of placing objects within our homes in the appropriate spots to best enhance the energy, or chi, within. For example, we will feel more secure if our desks are placed facing the door to prevent unexpected visitors from catching us unawares. A night table at each side of our bed invites a partner to share our lives with us. Fresh flowers in the house add a welcoming spirit, and the use of mirrors attracts light and good chi.

No, Jamie and I are not equating friends with the inanimate objects in our houses. But we do believe that arranging your life to include your friends will enhance your personal energy. The right friend will be there for you to assist when an unexpected event occurs. When she calls or meets you for lunch, her compassion can uplift your spirits if you are down. And like a mirror, she can reflect back to you the happiness you are feeling when life is particularly joyful.

The people who make a difference are not the ones with the credentials, but the ones with the concern.

—Max Lucado

Kristin has many friends in her life, but she is especially fortunate in one particular friendship. She and Susan met thirty-some years ago, back when they were both newlyweds and had moved to the same community. They met at the local gym and discovered an immediate affinity for each other. As they talked while walking on adjacent treadmills, Kristin and Susan discovered they shared many of the same likes and dislikes in music, food, and TV shows. Their similarities extended beyond the frivolous, however, for they were both small-town girls with comparable ethics and value systems. A camaraderie sprang up between them, and together they set about exploring the town, meeting other women, and finding outlets for their similar interests. Through the years, as they had children, began careers, and moved to different neighborhoods, their bond remained strong, even though their lives began to go in different directions.

They made time for each other, in outings that were sometimes planned, and sometimes spur-of-the-moment—the flea market, a bike ride, lunch at a favorite café. Other times they kept in touch through a phone call or a quick e-mail. How they connected wasn't as important as the fact that they kept in contact.

When Susan ultimately went through a painful divorce, she turned to Kristin for solace and words of wisdom. Three years later, when she remarried, again it was Kristin who was there for her, this time to share the joy of that wonderful day, helping her choose her wedding dress and prepare for the celebration. And it was Susan who could fully understand the depth of

Kristin's happiness when her son, who had always struggled through school, ultimately graduated from college with a degree in communications.

Whether living close by, or several states apart, Susan and Kristin were always present for each other with words of encouragement and support. Theirs was, and still is, the epitome of true friendship.

If we are lucky, we too have friendships like these in our lives.

There is a Broadway show called *Wicked*, which is based on a book of the same name by Gregory Maguire. It is the tale of the Wicked Witch of the West and her friendship with Glinda the Good. And it teaches us much about friendship.

These two women from different backgrounds, with disparate styles and value systems, ultimately form a strong, lasting bond.

They learn much from each other, whether they agree with each other's points of view or oppose them. In one particularly beautiful song they sing,

"I've heard it said that people come into our lives for a reason,
bringing something we must learn.
And we are led to those who help us most to grow, if we let them,
and we help them in return."

My own life experiences echo with the truth of this message. As all of us grow from childhood into our adult years, different friends join us on our journey through life. Some companions remain with us through all of our many transitions. Others might disappear at some point, sometimes never to cross our paths again. And, on occasion, a long-lost friend reappears somewhere down the road, completely out of the blue.

I have always been convinced that these friends are there at a particular time for a reason. They exist as role models for us to follow, or they need us to be role models for them; they are part of a support group we need to get through some of life's challenges, or they join our lives to share in overwhelmingly joyous occasions.

As in Kristin and Susan's example, a friend can be with you until the end. However, at times, the strong bond of friendship diminishes through the years, and the closeness begins to wane. This is natural: people change, and interests and lifestyles shift as people grow. Perhaps we just take these old friends for granted. Yet it is important to remember the roles that these women have played in your life.

Have you ever had an old friend suddenly say thank you for something you did for her in the past? It is possible that you didn't even recall the incident. Yet your friend not only remembered, but even went out of her way to express her gratitude. Obviously she had been thinking about the episode and wanted you to know she was still grateful.

Now put yourself in her place. Surely there was a time in your life when a friend's counsel helped you through a difficult situation. Even if she's a woman you haven't stayed in touch with, how wonderful it would be for her to hear from you. It would do you both a world of good—you for calling back to mind her loyal friendship, and her for the reminder that you still appreciate her.

To the women on my journey
Who showed me what I am and what I am not,
Whose love, encouragement, and confidence
Held me tenderly and nudged me gently . . .

—Rev. Melissa M. Bowers

Back to my friend Jamie and her theory of "friendship feng shui." She frequently uses the example of a beautiful chair that you were once given as a gift. You placed it in the center of your apartment's living room, next to a graceful table. A vase filled with water lilies was sitting atop that table, helping to make the chair a focal point of your room. As time went on, you got married and moved to a new home, and the chair found a place in your study. Eventually, it was tucked away into the corner of a guest bedroom. That is where it remains today, piled high with spare linens and a folded bedspread.

Once upon a time, you may have similarly taken delight in the beauty of a special friendship. You entered into this relationship with great enthusiasm; you laughed, shared secrets, advised and comforted each other, and even cried together. Yet time took its toll, and the two of you drifted apart—you lost sight of the unique qualities of that friendship, much as you lost the sense of elation you once felt in gazing at that beautiful chair.

If you uncovered that chair and removed the accumulated objects that are now hiding its beauty, you would once more be able to enjoy it as you once did, when it was the centerpiece in your little living room.

So too should you uncover the years and changes that have kept you from your old friend. Perhaps you don't see her anymore because you are geographically separated. And it is possible that you are worlds apart in your lifestyles now. But this doesn't erase the bond that you once had with each other. Certainly now, in this age of instant communication, you can keep in touch—just pick up the phone or fire off a quick e-mail.

Why not send her a message? See how she is and find out what her life is all about now. Let her into your world. This friend who was once such an important part of your everyday life is one of the reasons you have become the person you are today. As a supportive and encouraging part of the life you once lived, she helped shape you to become the woman who now inhabits your body, mind, and soul.

I'm not expecting that you two will instantly rekindle your close friendship. That may or may not happen. But what I hope that you will do is relive a bit of your shared past and find renewed comfort in those remembrances.

*Isn't it astonishing that all these secrets
have been preserved for so many years,
just so that we could discover them.*

—*Orville Wright*

I meet many women as I travel around the country. I bet you do, too. Have you ever noticed that on a long plane flight, the woman who becomes your seatmate for the journey is often eager to share her latest personal saga? Once I heard the entire story of a woman's recent breakup with her boyfriend. On another trip, I made the acquaintance of a woman whose only daughter had just gone off to college. This mother was excitedly detailing to me the plans she had to go back to school herself, now that she had the time.

I remember, in particular, a woman who was traveling back to her home in the Northeast after having spent the winter with her daughter Louise, down South. She had thoroughly delighted in spending the time with her daughter, son-in-law, and their three young children. And she was particularly proud of the life Louise had made for herself. This hardworking woman sitting next to me felt good about the fact that as a single mother, she had been able to provide for her daughter, encouraged her to go to college, and helped support her during those years. Her daughter Louise is now an RN, and she and her husband are raising their children with the financial security my seatmate had never been able to enjoy in her own life.

Then she looked right at me and said, "Would you like to see some pictures?"

Well, to be honest, my mind was already drifting back to thoughts of finishing the novel I was in the midst of reading. But there was no way I could decline. And so she proceeded to pull a huge, brand-new photo album from her carry-on case.

With each picture that she shared with me, her enthusiasm and joy grew broader and brighter. It was contagious, and soon I was delighting in the story of her daughter's success almost as much as she was!

This was a wonderful example of the comfort

women can find in each other. We don't have to know someone very long before we're sharing our life experiences. Some people are more open than others, but even if the other participant in the conversation is more tight-lipped about her own circumstances, she will usually be more than ready to listen to your story and offer advice or support.

Keeping this in mind, think back to the days when women met in small "consciousness-raising" groups. Back in the late 1960s, they gathered to discuss women's liberation issues. Coming from diverse backgrounds, they weren't necessarily close friends, but they shared a common goal. They were women facing issues that affected the female community, and they were there to support each other by word and deed.

Nowadays, woman still meet together, in book clubs, church or synagogue groups, and political or civic organizations and at ladies' luncheons. And somehow we realize that the conversation is diverted from the main topic to areas more personally affecting our lives. And we find ourselves very open and receptive to giving and receiving advice and support. I've seen women who had never met each other before join in on these dialogues, not in the least ill at ease. We form a sisterhood with each other that allows for such discussions to take place—whether we've known each other for five minutes or five years.

I urge you to return to the ideal of sisterhood that sprang up in the days of those consciousness-raising groups and meet again in small and intimate settings. Gather some friends, encourage them to invite others, and make a date to meet for two hours once a week. Even once a month is better than not at all, if your schedules do not allow for more time than that.

Pick a topic and explore that for the time you

have together. Each week, choose a "leader" who will make sure you don't stray from the subject. However, if other thoughts come out during the meeting time, have her write them down. They will become the topics for future discussions.

You will be amazed at how much women have to share with each other, and at how much being a part of the community of women enriches our lives.

Open yourself up to your friendships—both old and new. And get yourself out and meet new friends and acquaintances. Every woman who touches you is a positive influence on your life. Let yourself laugh and cry with each of them. Allow them to encourage and support you both when all is wonderful and when you are down. Be a part of this amazing group of people we can call our sisters and our friends. You will be enriched, I promise!

Do you follow the Tao of the Defiant Woman in treasuring your friends and the community of women?

1. **Think about a friend you have in your life now:**
   - Do you take the time to listen to her as she listens to you?
   - How can you show her how much she means to you?
   - What fun activity can you and she plan that would be special for just you two?

2. **Think of a friend with whom you have lost contact:**
   - Why not try to reconnect in some way and catch up with each other's lives?
   - If you parted ways unpleasantly, can you rethink the situation and reestablish a more comfortable relationship?
   - How can you let her know that her friendship meant a lot to you?

3. **When you have a chance to be with a group of women you have not met before,**
   - Will you take the time to listen to their stories and learn from them?
   - Can you open yourself up to them and share a bit of yourself with the group?
   - If you find one or some of these women particularly interesting, will you go out of your way to meet with them again?

Principle Four

The defiant woman seeks positive role models to help guide her and strives to be a like example for her daughters.

To the women on my journey who showed me the ways to go and ways not to go, to these women I say "bless you" and "thank you" from the depths of my heart.

—*Rev. Melissa M. Bowers*

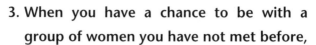

So often in our society, we find ourselves scrutinizing those we see around us. Perhaps it is conscious, perhaps not. A young and beautiful model in *Vogue,* the sad older woman who lives next door, our mothers or our daughters. Maybe a stranger caught your eye for some outstanding reason. Did you think, "I hope I never get that way?" Or did it cross your mind that this was a woman you would like to emulate?

It's human nature to look at others and compare ourselves with them. Sometimes we come out on the short end of the stick: I'm not as youthful, I'm not as slim, I'm not as bright, or I don't command the attention (e.g., The construction workers whistled at her; why didn't they whistle as me?). It's all so self-defeating. If you're short, longing to be tall like the model on the runway not only is a waste of time and energy, but also it keeps you from recognizing the beauty of your own petite frame.

The same can be said for the woman who has achieved a certain age, let us say sixty-two, and looks forlornly at the twenty-six-year-old in a miniskirt and tank top. Wishing herself back thirty-six years is just not productive—or practical. However, perhaps she sees something in that younger woman that she can incorporate into her life. Maybe there is a vigor, a joy of life, that emanates from the twenty-six-year-old that our sixty-two-year-old friend has lost somewhere along the way. Now, there's something worth noting—not that this other woman is younger, but that she appears to be filled with a vitality that has little to do with age and almost everything to do with attitude.

What all women have to cultivate is the ability to look at other women and recognize in them those traits that we would like to nurture in ourselves. What we need to find are role models—women who can help guide us along the path of life, defiant women who, by also following the principles of the Tao, can teach us te by virtue of simply being the people they are. With te, they are living their lives virtuously—skillfully.

Jennifer and her friend Lucy met two such role models while on a hike. Seven years before, at the wedding of a friend's son, they had discussed their various hiking experiences. Recognizing their mutual enjoyment of the activity, they had decided that they'd have even more fun if they participated in this pastime together. And thus began a once-a-week hiking tradition that seven years later, they were still continuing.

On one particularly beautiful fall day, Jennifer and Lucy were enjoying a moderately strenuous trek though part of the Appalachian Trail in Kent, Connecticut. As they climbed over formidable rocks and forged their way down the marked trail, the conversation turned to their first forays together almost seven years ago. And with Lucy soon to be celebrating a birthday, they commented to each other that they might just have to stop hiking one day. After all, as time passed, it would become more difficult to navigate such irregular terrain. For how many more years, they wondered, would they be able to keep up their weekly hikes?

This was by no means a heavy exchange filled with doubt and dread. These words were merely the musings of two active women thinking about their future. But Lucy was a bit more pessimistic than Jennifer. After all, she remarked, one day they might need to use canes to get around. They'd certainly be frailer. "Let's enjoy this while we can," she said, "because it isn't going to be forever."

Jennifer did not share the same glum attitude as her friend, but chose not to respond to this comment.

Shortly after this conversation, while following the path, scrambling uphill and down, they saw two women ahead of them. Both appearing at least a decade older than Jennifer and Lucy, these women were using canes for support. When there was a split in the trail, the women in front of Jennifer and Lucy took the easier of the paths, but what most stuck in Jennifer's mind was that the older women were out there. They weren't taking the more strenuous routes, and they relied on their canes, but they were hiking. The same canes that Lucy had assumed would keep her from hiking in the future were the canes that they utilized for support to help them continue enjoying this activity.

These women had unknowingly become role models to Jennifer and Lucy. Now Jennifer was able to respond to Lucy's dismal pronouncement, spoken earlier in the day. She pointed out the two older women in front of them and helped Lucy to see them as an inspiration rather than merely two feeble older women. And as long as they continued to hold on to the affirmative image of these two women hiking with their canes, Jennifer and Lucy had a good chance of remaining positive, active, and content as they continued on their journey through life's stages.

As we travel through life, we may indeed find ourselves fortunate enough to have role models who knowingly and willingly take on the task of guiding us. Our grandmothers, mothers, sisters, aunts, and cousins instructed us in how to behave, how to act, and even how to think and what to believe. Maybe there was an older family friend or a coworker who taught you how to conduct yourself in various situations.

And there were the never-ending announcements from your elders: "I look in the mirror and see an older woman, yet I still feel like a kid."

"How can you be upset about your birthday? You're still so young!" "Enjoy your life every day; you're never too old to have fun."

When you first heard those words, did they really sink in? Or were they merely just a bit of trivial rhetoric? You were so young, and they were so old; how could what these women said possibly relate to you? Now, however, as you reach the same stages of life they were enjoying back then, can you recognize the truth in their statements? And isn't it tempting to repeat these platitudes to your own children and grandchildren?

Picture, also, how these women showed you the way with their actions. Perhaps your grandmother loved to dance and continued to do so at family parties well into her older years. Now when you're at a wedding or bar mitzvah, can you picture her kicking up her heels and allow yourself to do the same, rather than sitting it out and saying that you're "too old to do that sort of thing"?

Our role models need not always be close friends or family members. Sometimes, as with Jennifer's and Lucy's fellow hikers, they appear almost for a nanosecond, but leave such a lasting impact that they remain with us forever.

Joanie met such a woman several years ago when she was working in a craft shop. One morning a customer entered the store—a woman who appeared to be in her seventies and who was sporting a baseball cap covered with buttons. There were buttons with cute sayings on them, buttons from various tourist sites, even buttons advertising her favorite sports teams. Upon complimenting the woman on her very unusual (and adorable) hat, Joanie was told, "Every child deserves an eccentric grandmother, so I decided to be just that for my grandchildren." And with that statement, the woman gave Joanie the most wonderful smile of pleasure. She certainly was relishing her role of eccentric grandmother!

Years later, when Joanie's daughter announced that she was pregnant, Joanie had a difficult time coming to terms with the fact that she would now be a grandmother—until she remembered that wonderful woman in the craft store with the button-covered cap. Okay, thought Joanie, if that woman could enjoy being an eccentric grandmother to her grandkids, so can I. Today, thanks to a chance meeting with a woman who became a strong and positive role model for Joanie, she is thrilled to be a grandmother—a very lively grandmother—to two active granddaughters.

The lessons of role models can work for us or against us, depending on our points of view. Two women hiking can look old and frail to us, or they can show us the way to continue enjoying life to it fullest despite physical restrictions. An unconventionally attired grandmother can look bizarre or wonderfully quirky and fun-loving. These women become our guides on the path of life and can help us, if we let them, enjoy every step along the way.

I'm sure you have heard the adages that there's safety in numbers and that misery loves company. Well, when you are going through a particularly difficult time in life, I do not expect you to draw comfort from the fact that someone else is in also distress. However, when you're in the midst of a personal upheaval, such as a divorce, it can be beneficial to look around for those who have faced similar problems. How have they dealt with them? Do you have a friend or acquaintance who has "been there, done that"? If so, hopefully you can draw strength from the fact that she has come out on the other side, one way or another.

For example, perhaps this friend has gone through a painful divorce. A spiritual and vibrant woman, she has emerged strong and independent. She now enjoys life as a single woman and continues to find joy in each day—now, however, with a different lifestyle. She has found more time for herself, has begun to develop skills she never knew she possessed, and has become more secure within her own being.

You might know another recent divorcée who, deeply depressed, has retreated into a shell. She finds no pleasure in her life and has a difficult time coping with the day-to-day activities of life.

If I were to ask you which of these two friends you would most like to emulate, I feel sure the answer would be clear, or at least, I hope it is. I trust you'd like to follow the lead of friend number one, who has learned to continue down her path with confidence and joy.

Then allow her to become your role model.

Surely this friend experienced many of the same painful feelings you are suffering now. But she didn't just pass through this dark tunnel overnight and come out the other end all brightness and light. It is even possible that she still has her gloomy moments hidden from view of others. Yet somehow, she was able to work through the challenges that faced her as she went through that divorce. And her Tao-and-Defiant attitudes worked together to carry her down that rocky path.

This is another example of the principles of the Tao of the Defiant Woman working together; this woman who is your role model is also your friend. You can draw from that special bond created by friendship and let her help you through your own divorce. Follow her lead. Watch her as she continues on her way. Allow her to give you support through both words and actions. I encourage you to let her become your role model. You will both benefit greatly from the experience.

> ✳ ***The first great gift we can bestow on others is a good example.*** ✳
>
> *—Thomas Morell*

And as we follow those who have walked the road in front of us, we too can become guides to women following us.

One day, you may even become a role model for that friend of yours who has decided to lose herself in grief and wallow in her new role of divorcée. Your example of strength might just help her come out of her dark shell. But please do not assume that I am telling you to march over to her house and impose yourself on her. Your effect should be loving and subtle, not forceful. Become that good example for her to see and for her to, hopefully, want to follow.

A wise woman I know once told me, "Remember, people will judge you by your actions, not your intentions. You may have a heart of gold—but so does a hard-boiled egg."

Encourage your friend by your actions. Not only will it help strengthen your soul, but it might just help hers as well.

In "The Real Woman Creed" Jan Phillips writes:

I BELIEVE THAT YOUNG WOMEN ARE IN NEED OF POSITIVE ROLE MODELS AND I COMMIT TO BEING AN EXAMPLE OF AUTHENTICITY AND SELF-LOVE.

Yet when I approached the subject of role models with a woman I know at a luncheon last year, her reaction was one of absolute astonishment. "I have no daughters. How can I be a role model?"

Anna had just come back from the gym

where, she told me, she had done her weight-lifting and aerobic routine. At forty-five years of age, she was still young and able-bodied, but was quite a few years older than several of the other women with whom she had been conversing at the fitness center. Wasn't it possible, I asked her, that observing Anna allowed those women to realize they could anticipate being fit when they reached that stage of their lives? If any of them were worried about turning forty, Anna, with her workout, might very well remain etched in their minds as a positive role model.

But for some reason, Anna was upset at the possibility of becoming a role model. This is not unusual, and unfortunately, I've encountered many other women who feel the same way.

"I hope I'm like you when I get to be your age" is not a derogatory statement, and we should not assume it to be and take offense. Please remind yourselves of your own role models. When you think of them, do you do so in a negative way? No, of course not. They inspire you, and you'd like to be "just like them" because you admire the way in which they conduct themselves. If you, then, become a guide for someone who has not yet gotten to your stage, and if she recognizes in you a trait that she would like to emulate—well, isn't that the highest compliment? And shouldn't you feel proud of yourself instead of insulted?

We need to recognize that we have an opportunity to guide others—women younger, women older, and women of our own age. We do not know whose lives we will touch, but by virtue of living our own lives fully and vibrantly, by following the philosophy of the Tao, and by proudly proclaiming ourselves defiant women, we send a message to others out there. And it is an unmistakably positive message.

If we are not more trustworthy models, younger women will look at our tired, angry faces and plunge themselves into the pursuit of youthful beauty denying they will ever be like us.

—*Nancy Friday*

Do you follow the Tao of the Defiant Woman in recognizing the importance of positive role models?

1. When you see a woman you admire,

- Do you focus on her physical appearance, age, behavior, or vibrancy?
- Which personal trait would you most like to emulate?
- How can you begin to incorporate this into your own life?

2. **Think about your mother and grandmother:**
   - What lessons did they teach you about accepting life's transitions?
   - Do these lessons work for you as you follow the Tao of the Defiant Woman?
   - If not, how can you change the lessons to better fit your lifestyle?

3. **What lessons can you teach another woman by virtue of the way you live your life?**
   - Can you show your daughter or a younger woman that we can be vibrant at any age?
   - Will your enthusiasm for life help another woman get past a difficult time in her journey?
   - Do you take pride in yourself when you are a positive role model to others?

Principle Five

The defiant woman knows that the world around her continues to develop and is content, because there is always something new and exciting to learn.

IT IS NATURAL FOR THINGS TO CHANGE,
SOMETIMES BEING AHEAD, SOMETIMES BEHIND.
—TAO TE CHING (ROSENTHAL)

Life was so much simpler once, wasn't it? There were no computers and digital cameras to force us to become electronically savvy. Only a few years ago, operating the television meant pushing the on-off button and turning the dial to one of four or five channels—well, it seemed like only a few years ago. Now we're practically required to take a course in electronic engineering just to work the multitude of remote controls necessary to operate our surround sound, VCR, DVD, and TiVo. Just going to purchase a TV means learning the difference between plasma and LCD.

Even the music on your radio is no longer the same. Gone is the day when you could turn on the switch and hear something recognizable, something you could sing along to. Have you ever tried singing rap? It just isn't possible, is it?

Let's talk about clothing, shall we? How many of us have worn the same outfit to eighteen consecutive weddings, just because we absolutely could not find another in the department stores that didn't make us look like we were wearing our daughter's prom dress? The styles we see on the mannequins at the mall all appear too short, too low-cut, too frilly, or, well, just not for us.

Well, here's a revelation: people have been

complaining about "these new complicated times we live in" since the beginning of time. The fact is, if you are fortunate to live long enough, you are going to see changes around you. And you can sit back and groan, or you can pick yourself up and use these innovations to your advantage. Just think about the technological advances your grandparents and parents have seen. The gadgets that you now take for granted were marvels to them. And they were faced with learning new skills in order to master these new-fangled inventions.

Similarly, our children have no qualms about using computers or cell-phone/PDA combination devices. They've grown up with such things being a natural part of their world, just as we have taken television and radio for granted. And, here's an eye-opener: our children too will one day be either shunning or embracing some new invention that comes their way.

NEVER BE AFRAID TO TRY SOMETHING NEW.
REMEMBER, AMATEURS BUILT THE ARK;
PROFESSIONALS BUILT THE TITANIC.

We discover, also, that as we continue down the path of life, our individual circumstances change: jobs and careers are altered, we move from one city to another, and we find it oh-so-difficult to let go of all things familiar and comforting.

Do you remember a Broadway show many years ago called *Stop the World—I Want to Get Off?* The specifics of the story are not nearly as important to reflect on as the title. How many times have we wanted to shout out just the same sentiment? We want things to remain as they have always been. The life we know is comfortable, and we don't want to have to deal with the upheavals that change brings.

Things just don't work that way in the real

world, however. Life is a series of transitions. If that weren't so, all would become stagnant and dull. The rule of the universe is movement, and you and I are a part of this movement.

YOU WILL LOSE TOMORROW
REACHING OUT FOR YESTERDAY.

Sitting around and obsessing over the past does nothing to help you today. This is not to say that you must give up all that is old and dear to you. It does mean, however, that you also need to accept the new.

I've met many women on my travels who find themselves facing retirement. They have been actively working at one job or another, have made a specific career the focal point of their lives, and now find themselves no longer capable of continuing in the same position. Some face mandatory retirement. Some have just become burned out and realize it's time to leave the grind. Some don't have the physical abilities or stamina required for their specific jobs anymore. In each case, these women have had to learn that these are life-altering events—not life-ending ones!

Bridget's husband, Jake, was offered a job in Chicago, and it was one of those once-in-a-lifetime opportunities that they both felt he should not turn down. The only problem was that Bridget herself had to leave her own position as vice president of a major marketing firm in New York City. This had been her career, and life, for the past twenty-seven years. Having no children, she had been able to completely dedicate her energies to her marriage and her work. The move was a wrenching decision for the two of them to make, but both realized it was the right choice to make. Bridget's firm offered her an extremely generous early retirement package, and the opportunity awaiting Jake was exceptional.

They sold their home in New Jersey and moved to Chicago, where Bridget busied herself settling in and decorating the new house. Ultimately, she met the owner of a neighborhood boutique that she patronized, and that woman invited Bridget to join the local book club. Her new life just took off from that point. She made friends, became involved in various charity organizations, and even began to work part-time in her new friend's boutique, employing her marketing skills to enable it grow. She also realized that she now had time for the yoga and piano lessons she had always contemplated taking, and she happily settled into this next phase of her life's journey.

Now this is not to say that it all came easily

and smoothly for Bridget. Sure, she was lonely for her old friends. Of course she missed her career, her old home, and New York City. But after several months of feeling sorry for herself, she came to the realization that being miserable was not the way she wanted to spend the rest of her days. And only she could decide whether she wanted to remain unhappy and lonely or begin anew with an equally full and productive life—only now in Chicago instead of New York.

HAPPINESS IS NOT A STATE;
IT IS AN ATTITUDE THAT WE CAN DEVELOP.

If you, too, are facing a major life transition such as Bridget's, perhaps this is the time to look at those new electronic advances and decide to learn about their use, rather than continue to be intimidated by them.

Go into a library and try to find a book on your own, using their new system, rather than immediately asking for help. No, you can't find a card catalog anymore, but truly, those computers are not all that difficult. And I bet that a librarian will be more than happy to give you your first lesson.

Now take it a step further and enroll in a computer class. You might find, as one of our friends did, that it is not all that tough to operate one. And she also discovered the world of e-mail and the Internet. Clara didn't want anything to do with computers—"Too much trouble," she said. "I'm just as happy making a phone call or writing a letter, or even looking through an encyclopedia for information." Well, you may feel overwhelmed when you are faced with a tremendous amount of new knowledge. But even the electronically challenged among us can eventually learn to do at least one task on a computer. That success might just lead to a heightened interest in learning more. Or not. Either way, you have opened yourself up to the possibility of becoming computer savvy. Perhaps in the future, your new skill will play an important role in your life.

Learn how to send and receive e-mail, and you will find that you can keep in touch with friends you rarely see in person. Of course there are still telephones and the postal system, but e-mail offers a faster and very efficient option.

Figure out how to navigate the Internet, and you don't have to lug out those heavy encyclopedias when someone asks you what song the Beatles first performed on an American stage.

And by searching various sites, you might even find yourself a new job, if that is your desire.

I have many friends who admit that they still

can't operate the television set in their family room. But one acquaintance of mine, a woman with two young granddaughters, was extremely proud of herself when she was able to operate a DVD player for the girls. So too were the girls, who sat there calling out, "Yay for Grams!" How about that for a role model for those children!

Did your mother or grandmother have a hard time accepting the washing machine and dryer? Do you suppose that they thought learning to operate these machines was too difficult and that they decided to instead continue beating their clothing against rocks, wringing them out on a wringing board, and hanging them on clotheslines to dry? And how about that new-fangled iron that didn't have to be held over coals to heat up?

How hard did you fight the arrival of the microwave oven? Or automatic transmission in our cars?

The advances that we might have such a hard time incorporating into our lives today can be just as helpful—if we stop fighting them and try to wrap our brains around this new technology. Perhaps we're just afraid that we can't do it. How silly. There's only one way to find out if we can indeed figure it out, and that is to try.

A ship in the harbor is safe,
but that is not what ships are built for.

—John A. Shedd

We were put here to participate in the world around us, not merely to observe. And that participation requires us to accept new developments, rather than look upon them with scorn and fear.

You don't have to conquer the computer or the new flat-screen TVs in order to recognize that there are cultural changes taking place all around you. Just turn on the radio and listen to all of the different types of music waiting to either assault or appeal to your ears and soul. Now think back to your teenage days and the music you loved at the time. Did your mother completely embrace rock and roll as you did? There you were, bopping around to the raucous sounds coming out of your radio or record player, and what was your mom saying? Perhaps it was something like this: "Shut that off and listen to real music." Hmmm. Does this sound familiar? Could you be guilty of the same sentiments when you hear your children listening to today's songs?

Certainly you do not have to embrace rap or hip-hop, but please recognize that many others do enjoy this music. Don't just throw up your hands and claim that music was better in the old days—because that isn't necessarily the case. It was just different back then. You always have the option to continue enjoying the familiar things that appeal to you. Like all parts of our cultural lives, however, musical styles change, and to reject this reality is to deny the continuum of life. Do you really want to see the same movies, hear the same songs, read the same books, watch the same plays, and view the same photographs and paintings over and over again? How wonderful that we have the ability to alter our styles and enjoy such a great diversity within these pleasurable activities.

All the art of living lies in a fine mingling of letting go and holding on.

—Havelock Ellis

Look at the latest clothing trends in the magazines staring you in the face as you wait in line at the supermarket. Some appear to be mighty frightening—do the designers honestly expect real women to wear those things? Sure, an outfit might look gorgeous on one particular actress as she struts her stuff down the red carpet at an awards show, but you know it would look somewhat less stunning on you.

Or strolling around the mall, you may notice that the newest styles seem diametrically opposed to your particular shape. Those sleeveless tops wouldn't flatter your arms, and the low-rise pants would only expose your slightly rounded tummy.

The main point to remember here is that you do not have to wear something just because it is touted as the newest and latest and greatest. However, rebelling against these styles by reverting back to the clothing you wore ten or more years ago is not the answer either. There also seems to be a movement afoot to have us dress a certain way at a certain age. Pick up a women's magazine, and you might very well find an article telling you "how to dress" at forty or fifty or sixty.

I, for one, don't agree with that attitude. I truly believe that women can and should wear whatever we are comfortable in. If we think it looks becoming, if we enjoy the feel of a particular dress, then that is what we should be sporting. It is, after all, our attitude that pulls a style off successfully. You might wear the most figure-flattering outfit on the planet, but if you don't feel great in it, it won't look good at all. If, on the other hand, your sense of style is one that you enjoy—you have fun wearing a certain look—then go for it. It will only enhance your inner beauty and help to bring that out into the world around you.

You need to remember that you do not have to enjoy or adopt every change out there, but by staying attuned to the latest trends and technological advances, you have the option to choose the changes that work for you. By hiding your head and avoiding these new developments, you do indeed become outdated. Just as the world around you would become stale without these changes, so would you.

You are constantly evolving as you move from place to place, as your jobs and careers change, and as new innovations spring up all around you. Some of this is for the good. Some of these developments are less welcome. But each change has taken place whether you wanted it to or not. As John Lennon once said, "Life is what happens when you are busy making other plans."

Did you really assume that everything was going to stay the same? You know that's not reasonable. And pretending that you have not been touched by altered circumstances is not only unrealistic, but also unfulfilling.

Let these changes become a natural part of

your life and enjoy them. Go ahead and fondly remember the old days, but accept the new and fully partake in all that is waiting for you. Let these transitions in as you continue down the path of life.

Do you follow the Tao of the Defiant Woman by finding contentment in the changing world around you?

1. **If you had to move to another city,**
   - Would you be able to see this as an exciting new adventure?
   - What steps could you take before the move so that you would not feel totally alone in your new environment?
   - How would you remain close to those important people you would be leaving behind?

2. **When the day comes that you find out you must leave your job,**
   - Are you capable of seeing this as the beginning of a new chapter in your life, rather than as the end of an old one?
   - Will you decide to try a new activity, if you have more free time now?
   - Can you see how the skills you have gained in the past can be used in your future?

3. **Everything familiar seems to be changing, and new technology is being thrust at you:**
   - Do you cringe at the music on your radio or accept it, learn a couple of country songs, and try line dancing?
   - Will you wear a new dress style suited to you, or will you stick with your old ones?
   - Are you secure enough in your abilities to try to learn a new technological skill?

Chapter 3

Accept What You Must; Rebel Against the Rest

We have just discussed the five principles that you and I need to incorporate into our lives in order to experience true contentment with each new stage and phase as it comes our way. These principles, which closely follow those of the Tao, while also encouraging a bold, defiant attitude, cover the gamut of life-altering events that cross our paths as our lives progress.

In calling upon our Tao philosophy, we do the following:

- We recognize that as all things in the universe change, so too do our bodies, and we accept and embrace this law of nature.
- We find ourselves dealing with evolving relationships within family and friendships, and we come to recognize the important places these people hold in our lives.
- We learn to become a part of the amazing

community of women that offers us immense support in times of both hardship and joy.

- We realize the significance of finding and being role models because, in doing so, we discover courage and strength.
- We know that new developments are thrust upon us on a daily basis—those we anticipate and those that seem to come out of the blue—and we use them to our benefit without clinging to the past.

Through all of this, we find several key ideas to help guide us along the journey. These strategies are not some big secret. You possess these powers already. The key lies only in the strength of your desire to unlock the powers that you already hold in your head, heart and soul, allowing them to lead you down the path. The choice is yours to make—whether you wish to wallow in defeat and sorrow as each new transition comes your way, or you wish to embrace changes and live your life joyfully.

WE HAVE BUT ONE LIFE—WHETHER WE SPEND IT LAUGHING OR WEEPING.

The Tao gives us the foundation upon which we can build our new way of living. Women truly need to understand those philosophies in which Taoism is rooted.

We have to remember yin and yang, knowing that all things depend on those opposing principles.

Remember you cannot have the beauty of great light without the presence of shadow. You cannot have the heights of happiness without the depths of sorrow.

—*Deborah Charles Wilson*

It is important to hold on to this concept; to remember that there need be the balance of yin and yang in our lives. It is with this knowledge that we can face disappointment, for we understand that having known heartache allows us to truly appreciate the joyous moments in life. I'm not saying that we must go out looking for the negative just to be able to enjoy the positive. What I am suggesting, however, is that we understand that life contains both joy and sadness, light and dark, health and illness. To deny this truth would be to refute the fact that the universe works because of the interaction of night and day, of winter and summer, and of paths that are smooth as well as rocky. With acceptance of the yin and yang comes a peace of mind that allows us to follow our course with all of its transitions and challenges: to take them as they come, deal with them, and know that another day and another change are waiting around the corner for us. Confront changes one at a time, have patience, and believe in the power of nature to bring us to the next day, the next stage.

As a Tao-and-Defiant woman, I hold on to the philosophy of *tzu-jan* and recall that the flow of nature happens by itself, without any prodding or planning from me. And, being a part of the universe, I, like you, find myself moving through these transitions as my life continues along its path. We have to accept the changes we see in our bodies, in our relationships, in the world around us. To deny these developments is to buck nature and create a block that is insurmountable and that will only lead to unhappiness.

✻I trust that everything happens for a reason, even when we're not wise enough to see it.✻

—Oprah Winfrey

We need to remember *wu wei* and avoid forcing issues, going with the flow to the best of our abilities. Only then can we turn a situation around and make it work for us. You can't open a door by jamming the wrong key in the lock. But find the right key, and that door will easily open wide and allow you through. Kicking and fighting our way out of a situation will never work. Trying to hold on to a love or friendship that we must leave, even after it no longer fits our lives, can only bring pain. But when we take that circumstance, learn whatever lessons we can, and then apply that knowledge to the next phase of our lives—well, now we're following the Tao and the principle of *wu wei.*

As for accomplishments, I just did what I had to do as things came along.

—*Eleanor Roosevelt*

Te is more difficult to describe. How does one talk about virtue without discussing a person who goes around telling everyone how good she is? That woman you might meet at a party, who eagerly details all of her hard fund-raising work—well, she is doing good things for the world, but she isn't exhibiting te or virtue, as it is meant by the Tao.

The attribute of *te* refers to being virtuous at the skill of living. A person demonstrating *te* knows who she is, accepts that, and does the best she can wherever she happens to be at the time. If we know our strengths and weaknesses, and we accept ourselves because of them and in spite of them, then we are examples of *te*. This is not to say that we give in to our personal flaws, but we do start with acceptance and build ourselves up from there.

The little girl you once were was happy to run down the street singing or to get up and dance to music that was playing on the radio. You didn't worry about whether you were good at these activities; you enjoyed them for the joy they added to your life. You accepted yourself without judgment—you were simply enjoying the fact that you were you. Somewhere along the line, we began to decide whether we were good at something. We came to various conclusions about how we looked, sounded, and behaved. As such, we were not following *te* and allowing ourselves to just "be." When we cast doubt upon our own beings, we hinder our ability to live our lives fully and joyfully.

To "accept ourselves as we are" means to value our imperfections as much as our perfections.

—Sandra Bierig

To live life following the Tao of the Defiant Woman means not only following the principles of the Tao, but also including within your mind and heart those attributes that allow you to describe yourself as defiant as well.

Women today need to retain a strength of mind that allows us to endure adversity should it come our way. We need a good dose of fortitude and determination to help us on our paths. Want to achieve a particular goal? Well, fortitude is the quality that will enable you to do so. Okay, so your first forays into learning how to work that new cell phone/digital camera combination didn't work. Giving up sure isn't going to do the trick. Keep plugging away, or try to find the right situation in which to learn this new skill.

This is the truth of all challenges we face in life: hanging in there is the way to go. Of course, sometimes all the effort in the world will not allow us to achieve a particular goal, but at least we gave it our best in those cases. And perhaps, in the process, we picked up some new skills that will help us in another situation down the road.

Anything's possible if you've got enough nerve.

—J. K. Rowling

We live our best when we are vital and active. No, we might not be able to climb a mountain or surf the waves of the Pacific. However, when we remain vital because of and in spite of whatever circumstance we find ourself in, that's when we are truly experiencing this amazing adventure called life. Those who follow the precepts of the Tao of the Defiant Woman remain active in body and spirit through all of our days—wherever we are on our journey.

If you're quiet you're not living.
You've got to be noisy and colorful and lively.
—*Mel Brooks*

Bouncing back from setbacks and remaining resilient is of utmost importance to those of us who follow the Tao of the Defiant Woman. Things won't always go smoothly for us. But giving up because of a setback isn't going to help move you forward down your path. You will remain unhappily stuck in one spot, denying yourself the opportunity to march on ahead. The path will continue and will bring with it more challenges and more joy. Forge on ahead and see what lies down the road for you.

Being defeated is often only a temporary condition. Giving up is what makes it permanent.

—Marilyn vos Savant

One attribute—the chief attribute—that will see you through all of your days and help you to live within the Tao is humor. Learn to embrace this sentiment from Ethel Barrymore: "A definition of maturity: the day you have your first real laugh at yourself."

Without humor we would not be able to face the challenges that confront us on a daily basis. The difficult aspects of life would become even more challenging. Like a young child who falls from a tricycle, you can lie on the ground and cry, or you can pick yourself up, laugh at the situation, and get back on that bike. Surely we've all heard that laughter is the best medicine. Well, this is true for all of life. It is laughter that gets us through the tough times, and we need to remember and hold fast to its healing powers. Even the Tao asserts the necessity of laughter in our daily lives.

IF THERE WERE NO LAUGHTER,
IT WOULD NOT BE TAO.
—TAO TE CHING

As we journey down the path of life, we will all experience the natural flow of the universe. We will face challenges in the transitions along the road, and we must, as the Taoist does, accept them. However, passivity is not the way of the Tao. Acceptance does not mean giving up or giving in. We must take these changes, embrace them as a necessary part of life, and become defiant, not by yelling and screaming, but by employing all of our strengths and positive attitudes in order to continue on our paths. This is the way to live our lives as happily and completely as possible—which is the way we were meant to live our lives. This is the way we follow the Tao of the Defiant Woman. It would be a shame to lose our one opportunity at this go-around. We live in the here and now, and this is our one chance. We need to make this the best life we can, savoring every possible moment of joy and fulfillment.

I've had a wonderful life.
I just wish I had realized it sooner.

—Colette

Follow the Tao.
Live as a defiant woman.
And start now!

Appendix

Planning a Tao-and-Defiant Gathering

Tao-and-Defiant Do's and Don'ts

The Tao-and-Defiant Blessing

Planning a Tao-and-Defiant Gathering

After meeting with women of varied backgrounds over the years, I have discovered that we all share many of the same concerns. I've also found that, regardless of our religion, ethnicity, or occupation, all of us are women first. We all face similar challenges and transitions as we follow the path of life.

I believe that meeting others within the community of women is vital to our well-being. To aid you in the development of these get-togethers, I offer some general guidelines that I followed in organizing a number of Tao-and-Defiant gatherings of my own.

I've discovered that there need not be a strict formula to the afternoon or evening, but the inclusion of some structured activities provides useful jumping-off points, allowing specific topics to find their way into the arena.

In one game I've led, women form two lines, facing each other. A moderator, reading from a list, poses a question to the group. Each woman has sixty seconds to respond to the woman facing her in the second line. Then, at the end of that period, the other partner answers the same question. The challenge here is to remain focused, talking and listening only to your partner and answering the question, when it is your turn, honestly and openly. The topics can range from such issues as "How do you feel on your birthdays?" to "What was the happiest time you've spent in the past year?" to "What woman in your life do you most admire?"

The amount of information that pours forth is amazing; from this, you can formulate a long list of issues for further consideration and discussion in meetings to come.

Playtime should always include magazines, crayons, scissors, and glue, just as this next activity does. With each woman seated in front of a blank piece of poster board, ask the women to create a map of their lives. This freewheeling exercise can assume any form that they want. Some women make a time line of themselves using pictures or text torn from the magazines and pasted on their board. Others choose to draw pictures from their past, present, and even future dreams. One woman might depict her most joyful experience, whereas another might show a particularly sad time.

After an occasional bout of reluctance, the women in attendance really get into the swing of this. I promise that you will be amazed that a time limit will have to be set, or the entire gathering will be spent on this one activity. And after all are finished, each woman will have a visual reminder of some part of her life that she will eagerly want to discuss with the rest of the group. These topics, too, will find their way into the growing list of subjects to be taken up at future meetings.

I'm also a big believer in the importance and positive impact of journaling. Therefore, I advocate some time be put aside at each gathering for some personal writing. You might offer a thought-provoking first sentence such as "I wish I could . . ." or "I am happiest when I . . ."

Photos are also great for inspiring ideas. Find a picture and ask the women present to write any short poem or essay that comes to mind when they look at it. The same goes for a provocative quotation that you might have read recently or have locked away in your memory.

These gatherings should not be overly structured. However, without any direction at all, you might find that you end up spending the hours talking about the latest reality show on television. Well, even that is okay if you can turn it into a conversation that relates to some of the challenges women have to face. But in order to keep the meeting from turning into a free-for-all, it really is important to choose someone to act as the moderator for the time you are together. A different moderator at each meeting would work just as well as appointing a single person to hold this post. This woman could come armed with some prepared ideas about what might be discussed during that meeting. It won't be difficult to find topics because each meeting will yield a wide variety of possibilities. An efficient moderator will keep the participating women on the subject at hand and will slate other subjects for later gatherings.

At all of the gatherings I have been a part of, either as attendee or as moderator, I have found one amazing fact to hold true: no matter where we are, women want to communicate. We need to share our thoughts and dreams and allow others to do so with us. Whether we are a group of women who have known each other for thirty years or recent acquaintances, we are open with each other. No one needs to be forced to "come clean" and share something about her life that she'd rather keep private. There will be more than enough information that is less stressful to contribute. Perhaps as time progresses, those topics that once were taboo will begin to comfortably come to the forefront.

We gain inner strength when the community of women unites. These women help support us when we are down and share our happiness in times of joy. We, in turn, have the satisfaction of knowing that we are there for our sisters, aiding them in their journey through life's passages.

Please, give this a try. Find four or five or ten friends and open your calendars and mindsets to allow for a weekly gathering. Ask them to bring friends of their own whom you might not have previously met. This is a promise that I make to you, right here, right now—and in writing: you will derive a world of pleasure and comfort from your own gathering.

Go ahead and plan your first Tao-and-Defiant gathering! Pick up the phone and start calling your friends right now.

Tao-and-Defiant Dos and Don'ts

As we travel down life's paths, we all encounter challenges and transitions specific to ourselves. Although women often share experiences, we also must deal with some that are ours and ours alone. I hope that by following the principles of the Tao of the Defiant Woman, and by recalling and utilizing the precepts of Taoism in union with those that characterize your defiant side, you are able to journey down your own paths with acceptance, joy, and vitality.

In an effort to further enlighten you as you adopt your own Tao-and-Defiant attitude and behavior, I offer the following guide:

Do	Don't
Look in the mirror and recognize the beauty of your smile lines, realizing that they are the manifestation of a joyous life well lived.	Immediately make an appointment with the local cosmetic surgeon.
Send your only daughter off to college with a kiss and words of encouragement, allowing her the freedom to become an adult.	Call your daughter at college on a daily basis to make sure she's doing her homework.
Allow yourself to feel the pain of separation after going through a divorce; then pick yourself up and begin a new life with determination and hope.	Give up on life.
Drive a friend to a doctor's appointment, because you know that friend would do the same for you.	Complain and feel put upon.

Do	Don't
Set aside time to have a weekly or biweekly gathering of women for support and camaraderie.	Say you don't have time and can't be bothered, missing out on a positive and uplifting experience.
Know that your actions are an example to other women and, by living your life according to the *Tao of the Defiant Woman*, become a positive role model for others.	Ignore the effect that your example may have on others.
Seek out women who are examples of strength and courage, and view them as models for your own life.	Gravitate solely toward discontented women, because, well, it's just easier that way.
Take continuing education courses to learn about computers, feng shui, or naturopathic medicine.	Don't try new things, fearing failure; anyway, the old and familiar has always been good enough.

The remainder of this page is blank; I've left it so on purpose. Perhaps you can fill in the space by adding to this list—but make it uniquely your own. What Tao-and-Defiant things do you do and feel proud of? And what actions do you find yourself engaging in that you can turn around into more positive behaviors?

Pick up a pen or pencil and start writing. Or, if that requires more energy than you care to expend right now, at least take some time to think about it. And while you're doing so, review the list I've created and see how you compare. You won't regret the time spent—it will go a long way toward helping you learn to follow the Tao of the Defiant Woman. And that, dear friend, is a very good thing, indeed!

Appendix

The Tao-and-Defiant Blessing

by Jamie Callan

May you look forward to the future,
and may you honor your past.
May you look in the mirror and
find the beauty in your imperfections.
May you feel the joy of your own amazing body,
and may you appreciate what your body can do
and forgive your body for what it cannot do.

May you accept the journey and know that all is
right with your world right now in this present
moment.
May you accept the mystery of tomorrow
and embrace the possibility of each new day.
May you wake up every day with a sense of adventure, and may you learn something new—each and
every day.

May you find the power to give yourself to this
world.
May you show the young the way,
and listen to what the old have to teach you.

May you find the strength to do nothing
when there is nothing to do.

May you open your senses to the exotic and new,
and may you remember and cherish the familiar.
May you look at yourself and the women around
you and see just how remarkable we all really are,
and may you recognize the true beauty we all possess—regardless of age,
and *because* of our age.

May you appreciate the gifts of time:
may you see joy and laughter in every wrinkle and
line and may you see the wisdom and love
and life well lived in every strand of silver.
May you celebrate your birthdays
and may you honor the gift of being here now,
having come all this way and
still being beautiful and full of life and
having so much more to give.

Bless you!

About the Author

Photo credit: Joseph Golden

Continually reinventing herself, CJ Golden has previously enjoyed careers in speech therapy, acting, and sales management. Now a freelance columnist, author, and motivational speaker, she shares her Tao and defiant philosophy with women everywhere.

CJ is also a regular contributor to the *Sally Jessy Raphael* TalkNet Show where she shares her thoughts and observations in a segment called "Golden Ponderings."

Residing in Connecticut, CJ greets each new day, challenge, and transition with her Tao and defiant spirit.